WORKING WITH ELECTRICITY

ELECTRICAL ENGINEERS

REBECCA ROHAN

PowerKiDS press.

New York

Published in 2016 by The Rosen Publishing Group, Inc.
29 East 21st Street, New York, NY 10010

First Edition

Editor: Caitlin McAneney
Book Design: Katelyn Heinle

Photo Credits: Cover Maskot/Getty Images; cover, pp. 4–29 (gear vectors) Hunor Olah/Shutterstock.com; p. 4 anyaivanova/Shutterstock.com; p. 5 https://upload.wikimedia.org/wikipedia/commons/5/5f/Benjamin_West%2C_English_%28born_America%29_-_Benjamin_Franklin_Drawing_Electricity_from_the_Sky_-_Google_Art_Project.jpg; p. 6 Monkey Business Images/Shutterstock.com; p. 7 pedrosala/Shutterstock.com; p. 9 (Samuel Morse) Everett Historical/Shutterstock.com; p. 9 (Alexander Graham Bell) https://upload.wikimedia.org/wikipedia/commons/1/10/Alexander_Graham_Bell.jpg; p. 9 (Thomas Edison) https://upload.wikimedia.org/wikipedia/commons/9/9d/Thomas_Edison2.jpg; p. 11 Chicago History Museum/Archive Photos/Getty Images; p. 13 Zack Frank/Shutterstock.com; p. 15 Ringlet/Shutterstock.com; p. 17 courtesy of U.S. Army Flickr; p. 19 Matej Kastelic/Shutterstock.com; p. 21 Kzenon/Shutterstock.com; p. 22 Hugo Felix/Shutterstock.com; p. 23 YORIK/Shutterstock.com; p. 24 Science Photo Library/Getty Images; p. 25 ullstein bild/Getty Images; p. 27 (top) science photo/Shutterstock.com; p. 27 (bottom) Andor Bujdoso/Shutterstock.com; p. 29 REMKO DE WAAL/AFP/Getty Images; p. 30 michaeljung/Shutterstock.com.

Library of Congress Cataloging-in-Publication Data

Rohan, Rebecca Carey, 1967- author.
 Working with electricity : electrical engineers / Rebecca Rohan.
     pages cm — (Engineers rule!)
 Includes index.
 ISBN 978-1-5081-4548-6 (pbk.)
 ISBN 978-1-5081-4549-3 (6 pack)
 ISBN 978-1-5081-4550-9 (library binding)
 1. Electrical engineering—Juvenile literature. I. Title. II. Series: Engineers rule!
 TK148.R62 2016
 621.3023—dc23
                         2015024933

Manufactured in the United States of America

CPSIA Compliance Information: Batch #BW16PK: For Further Information contact Rosen Publishing, New York, New York at 1-800-237-9932

CONTENTS

WHAT IS ELECTRICAL ENGINEERING?

Imagine a world without television, telephones, cell phones, or computers. Imagine a world without GPS systems, MP3 players, and even light bulbs. These items are just a few examples of the ways electrical engineering has shaped our world.

In 1752, Benjamin Franklin flew a kite in a lightning storm. Attached to it was a key, which became charged with the lightning's electricity. With this experiment, Franklin was one of the first to try to expand our knowledge of electricity. And that's exactly what electrical engineers do today.

Electrical engineering has been around since the late 1800s. Electrical engineers deal with the technology of electricity. They design practical, real-world devices that produce, **conduct**, or run on electricity.

Franklin was a scientist and inventor. His famous kite experiment was very risky. However, Franklin used his findings to create the lightning rod, which conducts lightning away from structures. This was an early example of electrical engineering.

UNDERSTANDING ELECTRICITY

It's important to understand electricity before learning about electrical engineering. Electrical engineers use the following concepts when they're designing and working with new electrical systems.

Electricity is a kind of energy. Electricity can build up in one place, which is called static electricity. Have you ever felt a shock while walking in socks on a carpet? When two things rub against one another, it causes static electricity. Electricity can also move, which is called current electricity. Electric currents power the electrical devices you use, such as televisions and microwaves. A circuit is a closed path an electric current can flow through. Electricity flows best through conducting materials, such as the metal copper. Electric motors are machines that turn electricity into movement. Motors power machines such as fans, motorcycles, and much more.

ELECTROMAGNETISM VISIONARY

Michael Faraday, a **physicist** working in the early 1800s, was the first to discover how a changing magnetic field's strength or position can create an electric current. Faraday discovered that if the magnetic field around an object stayed the same, an electric current wasn't created. However, when he changed the magnetic field, a current was induced, or created. The more a magnetic field changed, the higher the **voltage**. This was an important step in understanding **electromagnetism**.

Motion can be turned into electricity if you use a **generator**. A windmill is a good example. Wind moves the blades, which power a generator to turn motion energy into electricity.

THE HISTORY OF ELECTRICAL ENGINEERING

In the 1800s, the field of electrical engineering really took off. Electricity had sparked the interest of people across the world. The biggest developments of the time were the telegraph, the telephone, and the use of electric power and light in the home.

Back then, the study of electricity was considered to be a field within the study of physics. Yet the earliest electrical engineers came from very different backgrounds and ranges of study. Samuel Morse, the man who invented the electric telegraph, was an artist. Alexander Graham Bell—telephone inventor—dropped out of school at age 15. Thomas Edison was homeschooled. In the beginning, it seemed electrical engineers only required a thirst for knowledge and the ability to think outside the box.

Although he wasn't a scientist, Samuel Morse made huge contributions to the field of electrical engineering. He invented the telegraph.

IT'S ALL GREEK TO US

The ancient Greeks may have been the first to observe electromagnetic effects. More than 2,000 years before Ben Franklin captured a spark from lightning, a Greek philosopher named Thales of Miletus described a form of static electricity. He had noticed that rubbing fur on materials such as amber would result in attraction between the two. A couple of centuries later, Greek philosopher Socrates observed that a rock called lodestone not only attracted iron rings, but also passed on to them the power to attract other rings.

Alexander Graham Bell

Samuel Morse

Thomas Edison

THE WIZARD OF MENLO PARK

Thomas Edison was one of the greatest electrical engineers. His many inventions changed the world forever. Edison acquired a record number of 1,093 patents. He invented the phonograph, which reproduced sound, as well as an early battery similar to the type used today in digital cameras and MP3 players.

In 1876, Edison moved to Menlo Park, New Jersey, to build a research facility. He was known as the "Wizard of Menlo Park." There, he invented and patented a light bulb in 1879. He then founded the Edison Illuminating Company with the goal of powering and lighting the cities of the world.

Edison thought a direct current (DC) electrical system was best. He claimed it was safer than other forms. However, it only allowed for a power grid within one mile of the power source.

LIGHTING AMERICA

A major battle of electrical engineers occurred before the World's Fair of 1893 in Chicago. General Electric, Edison's company, offered to light the event, but at a high price. Then George Westinghouse, promoting Nikola Tesla's new **induction** motor, offered a lower price and won the contract. On May 1, 1893, President Grover Cleveland pushed a button and lit up almost 100,000 light bulbs across the fair. In this first large-scale test of alternating current (AC), Westinghouse and Tesla proved how electricity could light up America.

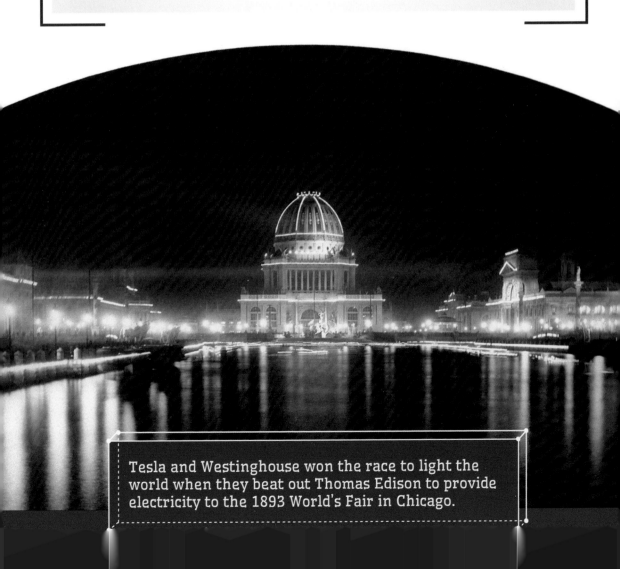

Tesla and Westinghouse won the race to light the world when they beat out Thomas Edison to provide electricity to the 1893 World's Fair in Chicago.

THE WAR OF CURRENTS

Tesla believed in using alternating current, while Edison believed in using direct current. Direct current always flows in the same direction between two oppositely charged places. Alternating current allows the flow of electrical energy to change direction. This is more practical for sending a great amount of electricity over long distances. The conflict between Edison and Tesla became known as the War of Currents. Tesla "won" the war when AC eventually replaced DC for power generation.

Tesla also discovered, designed, and developed ideas for several other electrical inventions. These included electrical generators and X-ray technology, as well as the rotating magnetic field, which is the basis of most AC-based machines. Tesla's 1891 invention, the Tesla coil, became the foundation for wireless technologies like radio and remote controls.

This statue of Nikola Tesla stands close to Niagara Falls, New York, where he designed the first hydroelectric power plant. This was the final victory in the War of Currents.

NIKOLA TESLA
INVENTOR
JULY 10 1856 SMILJAN YUGOSLAVIA
JANUARY 7 1943 NEW YORK

ELECTRICAL TERMS

Electrical engineers use many terms to describe electricity and its features. Many of the terms used in electrical engineering today come from the names of early contributors to the field. For example, the volt is named after Alessandro Volta—the Italian physicist who invented the electric battery.

The unit for measuring current, the ampere, honors French physicist André-Marie Ampère. Ampère founded and named the science of electrodynamics, now known as electromagnetism. James Prescott Joule developed the law of conservation of energy, so the unit that measures energy, or work, was named the joule. Finally, the ohm, the unit used to measure **electrical resistance**, was named for German physicist Georg Simon Ohm. Ohm's law describes the relationship between current, voltage, and resistance.

Electrical engineers have created many useful products over the past two centuries.

A TIMELINE OF ELECTRICAL ENGINEERING IN AMERICA

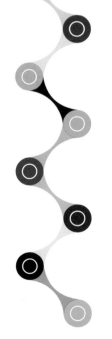

1844
Samuel Morse introduces the telegraph.

1879
Thomas Edison invents his light bulb.

1882
First commercial power plant opens in New York City.

1896
The first successful telegram is sent between continents.

1901
Guglielmo Marconi sends the first transatlantic wireless transmission using radio waves.

1919
Edwin Howard Armstrong develops the AM radio receiver.

1928
The first television program is broadcast in the United States.

1943
Work begins on the first general-purpose computer.

1954
The solar battery is invented.

1973
Mobile phones are invented.

1976
Apple I computer is released by the Apple Computer Company.

1989
First commercial handheld GPS receiver is released.

1994
Bluetooth wireless telephone technology is created.

2007
Apple Inc. releases the original iPhone.

PAST AND PRESENT

Electrical engineering has come a long way since the days of the phonograph and the invention of alternating current. Yet modern and future applications build on those same ideas. Communication systems are still important. Engineers work to improve the networks that allow instant voice and audio communication. They help the military develop reliable, secure communication methods for special force units operating secretly. They develop remote-sensing networks that can detect and **predict** earthquakes and tsunamis.

Just like the inventors of the late 1800s, electrical engineers design, develop, and test new electrical equipment. They try to solve problems. They still figure out the best ways of using electricity to transmit energy, but now they work on electrical systems on a much larger scale.

Members of the Communications-Electronics Research, Development and Engineering Center, or CERDEC, test a new communication system for U.S. Army vehicles in the field.

A CAREER WITH OPTIONS

A college degree in electrical engineering provides career opportunities in many industries. Electrical engineers work in the control rooms of manufacturing plants, space flight centers, and hospitals. They design and improve aircraft by installing more effective circuits and powerful computer chips. They work with computers and software, which of course are everywhere—our cars, homes, offices, and factories.

In recent years, electrical engineers helped invent DSL Internet connection, microchips, and solar panels. They've developed streaming video, home appliances, and computer games. The key industries that employ electrical engineers include aerospace, bioengineering, computers, education and research, energy and electric power, manufacturing, semiconductors, **telecommunications**, and transportation and automotive. As an electrical engineer, you can work in whatever field you're most interested in!

These electrical engineering researchers are working in a lab, observing a laser beam breaking on a glass surface.

A DAY IN THE LIFE

Unlike school, there's no such thing as a typical day for an electrical engineer. While many work in office buildings, laboratories, or industrial plants, others are based at construction sites, nuclear plants, or oil and gas production sites. They monitor or direct electrical operations and often solve on-site problems.

However, the skills needed for most jobs tend to be the same: the ability to design, implement, and test all or part of a given project. On a daily basis, electrical engineers have to come up with electrical solutions. They do this by trying to answer the question: "What does this need to do?" They have to test electronics and develop solutions to technological problems. They may have to help workers understand and use the finished product.

Troubleshooting electrical systems is just one responsibility an electrical engineer might have.

SPECIAL AREAS OF CONCENTRATION

There are many specialties in electrical engineering. Some electrical engineers focus on just one type of specialty, while others combine two or more. Here are some examples of different types of electrical engineers.

Electronic engineers design and develop electronic equipment and products. They create anything from GPS devices to smart TVs. Microelectronic engineers design and create tiny, electronic circuit components, or parts. They have to work with parts that are extremely small, and each movement has to be very exact.

MICROELECTRONIC ENGINEER

Some engineers work in the field of communication. Telecommunications engineers work on systems that send information through cables or fibers, which is important to telephone technology. Computer engineers design and improve computers and computer hardware.

Network engineers design and implement computer networks. They need a working knowledge of electrical concepts, tools, and safety.

BECOMING AN ELECTRICAL ENGINEER

If you're considering a career in this field, it's important to do well in high school science, technology, engineering, and math classes. You can get more education and experience by participating in activities such as science and technology fairs or robot, rocket, and electronics competitions.

The next step is earning a bachelor's degree in electrical engineering or a related field of engineering, such as electronics or telecommunication. In college, try to take as many science, technology, engineering, and math classes as possible. All these subjects are important for a career in electrical engineering. People who want to be more involved in research and development often continue their studies to earn a master's degree or higher. There are many different areas of specialization you can focus on.

COMPUTER SMARTS!

Today, electrical engineers rely more than ever on computers. They might use a computer program that **simulates** how an electrical system or machine will work. This is safer than doing an experiment without knowing what might happen. Electrical engineers might also use computer-aided design (CAD) programs. These computer programs help people make designs for a device or system. If you're interested in this career, make sure to pay attention in computer class!

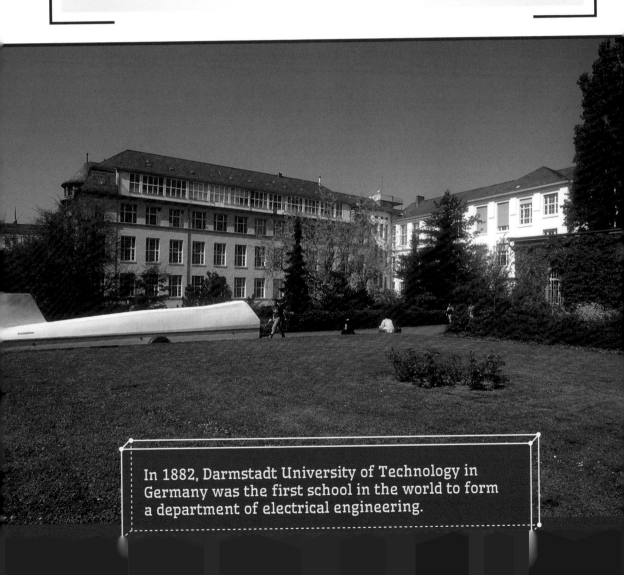

In 1882, Darmstadt University of Technology in Germany was the first school in the world to form a department of electrical engineering.

Electrical engineers today build on the advances and developments that engineering pioneers made long ago. At the University of Texas at Austin, electrical engineer Andrea Alù is studying and developing technology that can bend electromagnetic waves around objects so the objects are invisible to sensors. He also developed a device that breaks down sound so the user can hear someone talking, but can't be heard by others.

Michel Maharbiz, an electrical engineer at the University of California, Berkeley, is exploring ways to communicate wirelessly with the brain. This would allow some people who are paralyzed, or unable to move, to control the motions of their body. Other electrical engineers are creating smart robots that can locate survivors in earthquakes and accidents.

Robotics is another exciting branch of engineering that involves many of the concepts of electrical engineering.

Many of the ways we create electricity, such as burning the **fossil fuels** coal and oil, are harmful for the environment. Electrical engineers must look for cleaner sources of energy, such as solar panels, which turn the sun's energy into electricity.

Some engineers are looking to build highways out of pavement that acts as a solar panel. This pavement could also be used in parking lots, driveways, and streets so more clean energy can be made. Other engineers are developing "smart highways," which are interactive roads that can change the lighting and lanes to suit the conditions. Some highways may even charge electric cars as they drive. Future electrical engineers may develop new control systems for cars that drive by themselves.

In the near future, smart highways like this one in the Netherlands may become widespread, thanks to electrical engineers.

A BRIGHT FUTURE

In less than 200 years, electricity has become an essential part of modern life. Who can imagine our world without it? Electrical engineers work in multiple industries, including automotive, aerospace, defense, consumer electronics, lighting, computers, and communications. The government employs them in transportation departments, national laboratories, and the military.

Today's electrical engineers use basic tools and devices such as conductors, coils, and batteries that were invented long ago. In the 21st century, electrical engineers will lead the way in making necessary changes to our energy use and finding new methods of electrical power generation and distribution. They'll invent new ways to keep people safe and keep them connected. Our future is bright thanks to electrical engineers!

GLOSSARY

conduct: To allow heat or electricity to travel along or through.

electrical resistance: A material's opposition to the flow of electricity.

electromagnetism: The relationship between electricity and magnetism. A changing electric field produces a magnetic field, and a changing magnetic field generates an electric field.

fossil fuel: A fuel—such as coal, oil, or natural gas—that is formed in the earth from dead plants or animals.

generator: A machine that changes motion into electrical energy.

induction: The creation of an electrical or magnetic effect by the influence of a nearby electrical current or magnet.

physicist: Someone who studies matter, energy, force, and motion and the relationship among them.

predict: To guess what will happen in the future based on facts or knowledge.

simulate: To represent the operation of a process by means of another system, such as a computer.

telecommunication: Technology that deals with communicating at a distance, as with a telephone.

troubleshoot: To work to locate the cause of problems and make needed repairs.

voltage: The force of an electrical current.

INDEX

WEBSITES

Due to the changing nature of Internet links, PowerKids Press has developed an online list of websites related to the subject of this book. This site is updated regularly. Please use this link to access the list: www.powerkidslinks.com/engin/elect